THE KLUTZ BOOK OF
CARD GAMES
FOR SHARKS AND OTHERS

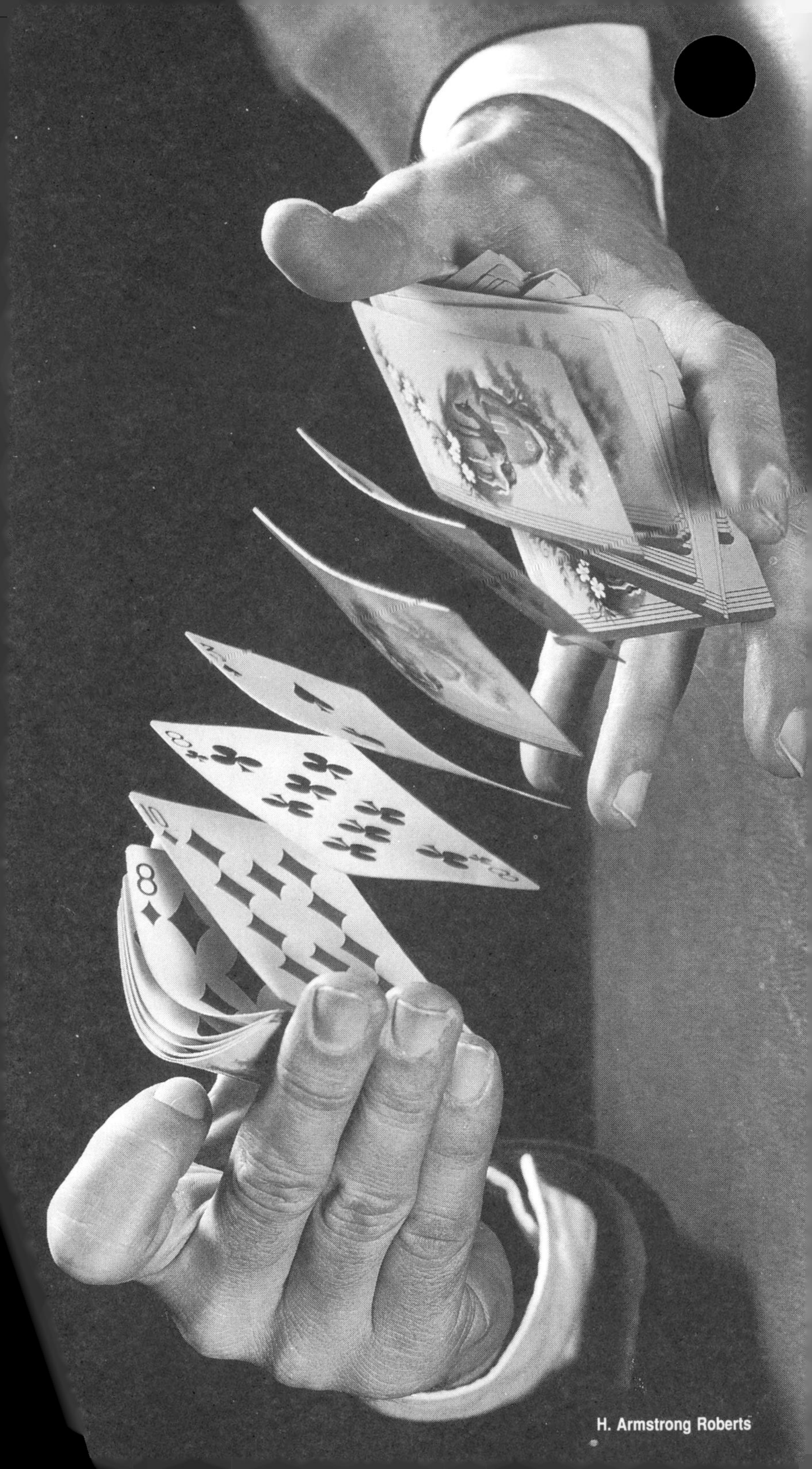

H. Armstrong Roberts

THE KLUTZ BOOK OF

CARD GAMES
FOR SHARKS AND OTHERS

♠ A compendium of
the 20 most popular
card games in the
galaxy, as well
as two knock-'em-dead
card tricks and
complete blueprints
to a three-bedroom
house of cards ♠

KLUTZ.

KLUTZ® is a kids' company staffed entirely by real human beings. For those of you who collect corporate mission statements, here's ours:

- Create wonderful things
- Be good • Have fun

Write Us
We would love
to hear your
comments
regarding this or
any of our books.
We have many!

KLUTZ®

455 Portage Avenue
Palo Alto, CA 94306

Book printed in USA. Cards printed in Belgium.

 The "book and bag" packaging format
is a registered trademark of Klutz.

Distributed in the UK by Scholastic UK Ltd.
Westfield Road, Southam, Warwickshire
England CV47 0RA

ISBN 0-932592-69-4

4 1 5 4

Visit Our Website
You can check out all the stuff we make, find a nearby retailer, sign up for a newsletter, e-mail us or just gooof of!.

TABLE OF CONTENTS

WHO INVENTED CARDS?

Nobody knows. But, whenever the origin of something is remote and mysterious, it has been traditional to suspect the Devil or Asia. This is particularly true in the case of playing cards, where the associations with gambling and idleness all but seal the case.

Of course, there are those who disagree. Other theories that surface from time to time identify the source as Egyptian, Spanish, Moorish, Saracen, Gypsy or French. The beauty of these theories is that, armed with nothing but a complete ignorance of any historical fact, one can wade boldly into the middle of a comparative discussion of any of them with absolutely no fear of ever being proven wrong or right.

We are, however, on firmer footing when it comes to identifying the source of the phenomenal popularity of cards. For that we have to thank Saint Bernard of Siena, a Franciscan friar from Bologna, Italy, who, in a fiery sermon in 1423, firmly identified Satan as the source of playing cards and playing card games. His cry was taken up on pulpits throughout the Church with the predictable results.

In 1576 the pastime got another boost when John Northbrooke, an English cleric, connected "wantoness, sloth, Ydolatrie, blasphemy, confusion and lust" with the playing of card games. Soon thereafter, a proclamation demanding that all "Cards, Dice, Tables and Bowles be Taken and Burnt" was duly issued. However, as a writer of the time briefly observed, it was a proclamation that "small Tyme endured."

Today, more than 175 million decks of cards are manufactured annually in this country alone, while worldwide, the playing of cards is generally acknowledged as the most popular game activity of all Tyme.

The look of the modern 52-card deck appears to come from either Spanish or Italian sources. After a stopover in France, this design—four suits of 13 cards each—began cropping up in England sometime around the end of the fifteenth century. Since this coincided neatly with the discovery of the New World, it seems quite possible that within the very first wave of European settlers to our own American shores, the Indians could probably have found a few card sharks (adding insult to injury).

GOOFENSPIEL

♠ Easy, easy, easy

♠ Two or three players

People who are good at this game think it involves a great deal of psychology—knowing how to read other people, especially their fears and insecurities. For these people, it is a game of depth and challenge. For others who lose at it all the time, it is all luck. For me, when I play it, I keep thinking of the scissors, paper, and rock game. Judge for yourself.

Separate the deck into its component suits, four little piles. Give one of the piles to each player and one to the center of the table (well shuffled). If you're only playing with two, put one pile away.

Each card is rated with points as follows: ace is high, worth 14 points; king is next, worth 13; queen is next, worth 12; jack is next, worth 11 . . . and so on. Suits are irrelevant.

Turn over the top card on the table's pile and examine it closely. You want this card because it's worth points. How badly you want it depends on how many points it's worth.

Now look at the other player(s). They want this card too. Once you've decided how much the other player(s) want this card, take one of your cards and lay it face down on the table. Everyone will do the same. (Basically, you're bidding for the card.) On a signal, everyone will reveal the cards they have bid. Whichever card is higher takes it.

The trick is to lay a card down that beats everybody else—but just barely. Incidentally, in the case of a tie, leave the turned-over card on the table, take back your played cards and try again.

Example: A 10 has just been turned over, worth (unsurprisingly) 10 points. You've sort of paid attention and think that the other guy has already played his jack. Not only that, but the king and ace are still in the pile, you're sure of that, so you'll have to keep some big guns in reserve to get them. In the meantime, how big a card do you lay down to get the 10?

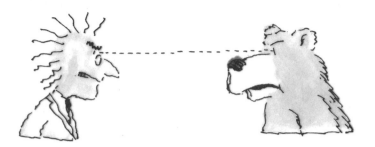

Look at the other player and give him or her a look that says the following: "You poor fool. I can read you like a book. No matter what you play, I'll beat it by one." That should give him pause. Then you recall he's lost the last couple of cards. He's probably desperate. The question is, will he play his queen? If he doesn't play his queen, will he just concede the card and throw off a trash card?

After staring at him for another hard moment, you decide that he can't bear to lose this card, so he'll play the queen. You play your queen as well in order to tie. Sure enough, you read him perfectly.

In the case of a tie, both players withdraw their cards and try again for the same turned-over card.

This time you raise the stakes, figuring he'll do the same. You play your king. He does the same. Then you take the big chance. You play a 2, he plays his ace. Congratulations. You've flushed 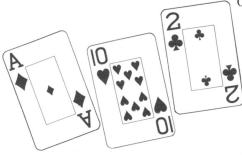 out his ace, all he got was a 10, and more important, his nerves are now completely shot.

WAR

- ♠ Easy, easy, easy
- ♠ Two, three or four players with one deck

This is the easiest game in the book. All you have to know is that ace beats king, king beats queen, queen beats jack, jack beats 10, 10 beats 9 . . . and so on. You can't be a kid without learning how to play this game. It's traditional.

BEFORE YOU START

The most common way to play this game is with two players, but three or four work as well. The object of the game is simple—collect all the cards. Here's how it goes: Shuffle the deck, cut it in half (exactly) and each player puts his half-deck face down in front of him.

THE PLAY

On a signal, both players turn their top cards over. Whichever card is higher wins. The winner takes both cards, puts them on the bottom of her pile, another signal is given, and the two top cards

are turned over once again. Whoever wins takes
those two and so it goes... until two cards are
turned over that are identical. When that happens,
it means War!

Here's what you do. The two identical cards
are laid side-by-side on the table, face up. On a
signal, each player reaches for their pile and puts
a second card—face down—on top of their matching cards. Then, on another signal, each player
puts a third card on top—but this card is face up
and compared to the other player's. Whichever is
higher then takes all six cards. If neither card is

And the 7 takes it.

9

higher, if you've matched cards again, it gets serious. You have to go to Double War! *Two* cards go

Double War

face down, the third goes face up. Whoever wins that match then takes all 12 cards! (If nobody wins the Double War match, you'd have to go to Triple War . . . three cards face down before one is turned up, but this is almost unheard of.)

If you're playing with three, start by removing one card (it doesn't matter which) from the deck. All three players turn cards over at the same time. When you get matching cards between two players, they go to War.

If you should get a match between all three players, you have to go to Double War right away. For four players, the rules are the same, except you have to decide before the game starts when you should go to Double War.

EGYPTIAN WAR

- ♠ Almost as easy as regular War, but more interesting

- ♠ Two to five players

This game is traditionally played on lunch or picnic tables, when you're supposed to be taking your tray back. The object is to collect all the cards. A single deck is dealt amongst all the players. The player to the dealer's left begins by turning his top card over in the "battleground," the center of the table. The next person turns his card over, puts it on top of the previous card, and round and round it goes. Make sure everyone puts their cards onto this pile snappily. No dawdling and no peaking.

When someone turns over a face card (jack, queen, king, ace), he or she can almost take the whole pile.

I say "almost," because the next person still has a chance. Let's say a king has just landed on top of the pile, and the king's owner is ready to grab the whole stack. If you're the next person in line, you get three chances to top him by landing your own face card (any face card, it doesn't matter which) on top of the king. You lay your next three cards on top, one at a time, and none of them are face cards. You lose. The king's owner grabs the whole stack and you start the next round.

Here's the pile...

You land a king...

And the next player fails to top it in three tries with another face card

The number of chances a player gets to top a face card depends on what the face card is. If you're trying to top an ace, you get four chances. A king, three chances. A queen, two chances. And a jack, only one chance.

But let's back up and change things. Let's say you *were* able to land a face card on top of the king. Let's say your second turn-over card was a queen. Now you can almost grab the whole pile.

Why almost?

Because the person after you still has a chance. You landed a queen? The next person in line gets two chances to top you with another face card. If they can't do it, you get the whole pile. If they *can* do it, they can almost take the whole pile. (Why almost? Because the person after them still has a chance...)

Now for the last important rule, slapping. If two identical cards are turned over—one right after the other—then the first person to slap their hand over the pile gets to keep the whole thing. The slapper can be anyone playing. This is one of those rules designed to keep you on your toes. Note that you can slap anytime two identical cards are turned over, even when someone is trying to top a face card. Here's an example of that.

A slappable pile

Let's say a queen has landed on the pile. The player after the queen's owner gets two chances to top it. But the first card turned over is a queen too. Whoever gets their hand down on top of the pile first, claims the whole thing.

If you make a mistake and slap when you can't, then you are penalized and have to take a card from your own pile and put it at the bottom of the discard pile.

If you run out of cards, you're out of the game.

However, all is not lost. You can still come back from the grave by "slapping in." You have to sit with your hands underneath the table, but if two matching cards turn up one after the other, and you can get your hand on top of them first—take the pile, you're back in the game.

CONCENTRATION

♠ Easy, easy, easy, easy

♠ For any number
with one deck

Of all the card games ever devised, Concentration might have the distinction of giving the smallest role to luck. If you have a photographic memory, this is going to be your game. Even if you don't, though, Concentration is an incredibly easy game to learn and good for groups that can't find a single game that everyone knows.

BEFORE YOU START

You can play Concentration on a table, but it works particularly well on the floor, since you'll be needing a lot of spread-out space. Take your deck and put each card, face down, on the floor (or table). Try to keep all the cards separated, not touching one another.

THE PLAY

The first player turns up one card, leaves it up, then turns up another. If they match (sheer luck) she gets to keep them both. If they don't, she has to turn them both back down. A "match" is two cards of the same value—they can be either color.

The next player is also looking for a match and he does the same, turns up one card, then another. Of course since he is going second, he has the advantage of having seen what two of the face down cards were. And if he can remember that piece of information, he can use it if the first card he turns up happens to be a potential match. If he can produce a match, he can take both cards away, and keep his turn.

When all the cards are finally taken, whoever has the most is the winner.

As play continues around the table, the memory pain can get pretty serious. The winning strategy is to remember as many of the cards as possible—what they are and where they are. Most people play so that cards are never shifted around. You turn a card up, then turn it back down without moving it. However, you can, if you really want to make everyone's brains start to hurt, permit players to move each card when they turn it back down.

I DOUBT IT

♠ Easy, easy

♠ Up to five players with a single deck; up to ten with two decks shuffled together

♠ A great game—one of the very best—for groups of mixed ages and mixed card experience

To win at this game, you have to be able to look your friends straight in the eye, give them a big smile, and lie like a dog. Keep that in mind and you should have no problem.

BEFORE YOU START

Sit everybody down at the table. Let's make you the dealer. Start, as usual, with the person to your left. Deal him a card and continue around the table until all the cards are dealt out. Don't worry if somebody ends up with a different number of cards. It doesn't matter.

The object of the game is to get rid of all your cards. First one to empty his hand is the winner. Here's how you do it.

THE PLAY

The player to the left of the dealer goes first. He or she always begins the round by laying down aces, as many as they have, face down. As they do that, they have to announce their play. They've laid down one card? They'll put their hand on a Bible and solemnly declare:

"An ace."

This could be a patent lie. In fact, it probably is. If anyone else at the table wants to challenge, they just holler "I doubt it!" (If more than one holler at the same time, the nearest hollerer wins.) After a challenge, the card(s) are turned over and one of three things happens:

1. It's not an ace. In which case the player who laid it down has to take it back.

2. It is an ace. In which case, the player who doubted it has to take it.

3. It's an ace, but there's another card hiding underneath it. In which case, the cheat has to take them both back.

The play continues around the table clock-wise. The next person has to lay down 2s, as many as they have, the next person 3s, the next person 4s, etc.

That's the way it goes. The player who lays her cards down can lie about what they are, as well as how many there are. She can set a neat little stack on the table, lean back and vow there are three kings in that pile. In fact, there may be one 5, two jacks and a single 3, but that's the beauty of lying. And note this: Nobody can touch the pile unless they put themselves at risk by first saying "I doubt it."

Speaking of risk, there's one more critical rule to bear in mind, which I'll illustrate as follows:

Let's say that someone lays down a couple of cards that no one challenges. Those cards stay on the table and become part of the "risk pot." If the next player is challenged, whoever loses that challenge has to take *all* the cards on the table. This rule is designed to give potential challengers food for thought.

What They Claim   **Hard Reality**

STRATEGY

I Doubt It is a rarity, a fairly tricky little card game disguised as a straight-ahead kids' game.

On the first level is the Hollywood stuff. You have to look like you're a dishonest liar when you're not, and then, a moment later, to look like you're telling God's own truth when you're lying through your teeth. You should practice whichever of these two modes is most difficult for you. Incidentally, it's not that long a reach between a good player of I Doubt It and a good poker player.

On the second level is the card planning. Arrange your hand so that everything is in the order you're going to need to play it. That should help you see how soon you're going to have to bluff and with what cards. Also, it pays to do your cheating early, before the pot gets very big; and it pays to get rid of cards that you know you won't be able to play legally.

If the top half of your hand has got a lot of holes (no high cards), and it looks as if you'll be forced to do a lot of lying in the later, dangerous stages, you can try to fill those holes in by doubting those cards if they're played early on. If you lose your challenge, you end up with cards you wanted anyway.

One final note. Most people play that you *have* to lay down a card every time it comes around to your turn. Others allow one, two or three passes per game. It's up to you.

THE BASIC RUMMY IDEA

On the *All-Time, Card Game Hit Parade,* Gin Rummy would have to rate somewhere in the top five. Since about 1930, when the film industry unofficially adopted the game as the standard backstage and between-takes filler, it has attracted millions and millions of players. It is, by some estimates, the best two-player game alive. (Although rummies can be played with more than two, it's not their best form and the descriptions below are tailored for twosomes.)

Hundreds of card games exist in the rummy family, all of them sharing a good number of family traits (understandably so, since they've all descended from the Spanish card game "Conquian," popular about 150 years ago).

The games vary a good bit in their need for strategic planning, with Gin Rummy, the best known, occupying a spot close to the top. None of them are terribly hard to learn though, at least not the fundamentals, and the three varieties described here differ less in that regard than they do in the demands they place on your craftiness and memory for cards played.

Rummy is a game where neatness counts. The object is to take all the mixed-up cards you've been dealt, and sort them into tidy combinations. If you can organize your hand in this way—or nearly organize it—you can "knock," or lay it down. When someone knocks or "goes out," the hand is over for both players and is scored. Don't worry if some of this is going over your head, it'll all make sense when you read the directions for the individual games. This is just to get you oriented.

In order to help find fitting cards, you're per-mitted to pull new cards as the game progresses. These combinations you're looking for (call them "melds") are quite simple, and come in only two flavors: straight flushes and several of a kind.

A straight flush might be the 5, 6, and 7 of diamonds, or the ace, 2 and 3 of hearts. As long as the cards are in sequence, as long as they are all of the same suit, and as long as you have at least three of them— you've got a straight flush meld.

"Several of a kind" is just what the name suggests. All you need are cards that match: three 7s (or four of them, if you're so lucky), or three 2s, or three kings... whatever. Note that you need at least three cards. A pair won't do it.

In rummy, the ace is traditionally the low card and fits with the 2, not the king. For example, the queen, king and ace do not make a meld. The ace, 2 and 3 do.

Here's how the play generally goes. The cards are dealt to the two players. The non-dealer gets an extra card, one more than the dealer. Both players look at their cards and sort them into melds or "suspects." Suspects are "maybe melds," melds that *may* come to be, depending on what cards get picked up along the way. A pair becomes a suspect for a "threebie," for example, and two same-suit cards in sequence are suspects for a straight.

Occasionally, one card may be particularly suspicious; it could fit into two possibilities, a possible straight, or a possible threebie.

Cards like these, that could go in either of one or two ways, are inserted between the two suspect melds when the hand gets organized.

A typical seven-card hand, after organization. Not too exciting. Note the placement of the 7 of spades, it's doubly suspicious. It could go with either a straight flush meld (along with the 8 of spades) or several of a kind (if you can find a third 7)

Despite the fact that it seems like tedious housekeeping, this sorting business is important. Spend a minute doing it.

After both players have tidied up their hands like this, it's the non-dealer's turn. He got the extra card, and he has to get his hand down a card. In order to accomplish this, he picks out the card that he likes the very least, and puts it face-up right beside the deck in the center of the table. By doing this, he starts the stack of discards that will be used for the rest of the game.

Now it's the dealer's turn. She can pull a new card (the top one) from either the face-down center deck, or she can take the card that her opponent has just put beside it face-up. Whichever card she chooses, once she's taken it, she'll have an extra card in her hand and she, too, will have to take one out. Whichever card she chooses goes in the face-up stack that her opponent began.

Back and forth, this is the way it goes. Each of the players pulls a new card—from the top of the stockpile or the top of the discard stack. They can either reject the card they pull, or keep it and discard some other card in their hand. As they get cards that fit into their melds, they should re-sort their hand appropriately.

At this point, the rules start to diverge a good deal depending on the variety of rummy being played. If you're new to the game, probably the best one to start with is called...

NO KNOCK SUMMER CAMP RUMMY

This is the fundamental rummy game. It contains all the essentials of any of them, but without some of the quirks of its more devious cousins. Before you start on it, read the preceeding five pages.

You're back? Fine. Deal seven cards to yourself, and eight cards to your worthy opponent. Lay the balance of the deck in the middle, between the two of you, face down. This is your stockpile. Sort your hand as he does the same. When he pulls his reject card, he should lay it face-up beside the center deck. It becomes the foundation of your discard pile, and now it's your turn to take a card and reject a card.

As you start building melds, keep in mind the following key rule: You cannot go out (lay your cards on the table, face up) until you have every-thing melded. In the jargon of the game, when you go out, you can't be holding any "deadwood," i.e., cards that are not a part of a meld.

Since you're reading this book, let's assume you're the winner. You've gotten all your cards into neat and tidy melds and you lay them down on the table smugly. Here's how you score.

Your opponent has to put all of his cards face down as well. Any cards that are in melds are put to one side. His deadwood, is counted according to the following scheme:

♠ Face cards count 10

♠ The ace counts 1

♠ Everything else counts the way it looks (the 6 counts 6, the 8 counts 8...)

Once you've finished counting up his dead-wood, put that number under your name on the scorecard. First one to 100 (or 500, or...) is the winner.

POP QUIZ

Q: How many deadwood points are in this hand?

A: 10

KNOCK RUMMY

Now it gets a little more serious. With Knock Rummy you can go out before you've completely melded your hand, as long as your deadwood count is less than 10 points. Also, you're working with ten cards each, rather than seven.

The extra cards, and the option of knocking, team up to add a thought-provoking degree of complexity to the game. Plus, the scoring is a little trickier.

When someone knocks, he should lay down his melds and deadwood separately, announcing his deadwood count (has to be under 10). The other player does the same. If they turn out to have fewer deadwood points than the knocker does, or even if they turn out to have the same number, then *they* win the hand.

This little business is called "undercutting" and it is rewarded with a 10-point bonus on top of the difference in deadwood counts. (I knock with 8 points? And my opponent lays down his cards to reveal only 4 unmelded points? He wins the hand by a total of 14 points.)

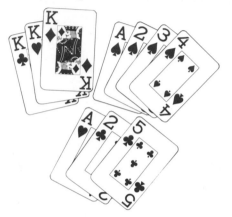

This hand knocks with 8 points...

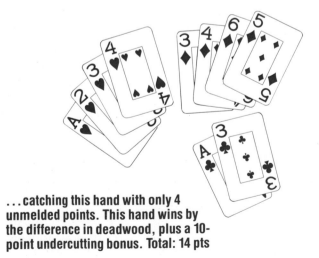

...catching this hand with only 4 unmelded points. This hand wins by the difference in deadwood, plus a 10-point undercutting bonus. Total: 14 pts

Undercutting is a little uncommon, however, and usually the hand is scored simply by taking the difference between deadwood counts. (I knock with 8 points? And my opponent lays down his hand to reveal 25 unmelded points? I win the hand by 17 points.)

This hand knocks with 8 points...

...but this time the other hand is caught with 25 unmelded points. This hand loses by the deadwood difference, 17 pts.

One last point to the scoring: If someone goes down clean, with no unmelded cards, that is rewarded with 25 bonus points on top of the deadwood difference.

Winner is the first to get to a pre-agreed goal, say 500 points.

GIN RUMMY

Once you've started to figure out the simplified rummies, you might be interested in the wrinkles that this last version presents. It is quite similar, except for the scoring, to tournament Gin Rummy.

The basic play is identical to Knock Rummy. Ten cards are dealt to the dealer, 11 to her opponent. Cards are drawn and discarded in the same way, and you can't knock with 10 points or fewer.

The biggest difference comes at the point when someone goes out and lays down their cards. In the simpler versions, when someone went out, her opponent was left with whatever deadwood she had and that was that. In this version of Gin Rummy, however, she still has an opportunity to get rid of some of her deadwood by laying it off on her opponent's cards. This little change was put in to give the underdog a final chance to bite back.

Let's say you go out with 6 points deadwood. It's a good knock and you're feeling pretty cocky. But your opponent happens to have a card that fits into one of your melds. (You've laid down a threebie of 8s? And your opponent is holding a lonesome 8 of her own? She can poach off you by putting hers with yours to make a foursome of 8s.)

Doesn't seem fair, does it?

Note, though, that she can't make any use of your deadwood. Those cards are truly dead. But, any cards that she is able to lay off do not count against her when the hand is scored and her deadwood is totalled up.

For example: You knock with 6 points deadwood. Through pure luck she is able to lay off an 8 on one of your melds. The rest of her cards are already melded except for a 3. That means you've been undercut. You went out with six cards, she got her hand down to three. She takes the difference in points (3, in this case) plus the 10-point undercut bonus.

If you want to completely avoid this unpleasant (but unlikely) scenario, you can try to go out clean (declare "gin"). When you lay down nothing but melds, your opponent is not permitted to lay off anything. Whatever her deadwood count is, add that to 25 (your gin bonus) and put that total under your name.

GIN RUMMY STRATEGY

Despite first impressions, Gin Rummy is a game that keeps the luck factor on a very tight leash. It is, in fact, a game that demands a high level of memory and devious thinking in order to consistently win. The following is gin strategy in a nutshell. Experience will take you further down the paths that these pointers are only meant to suggest.

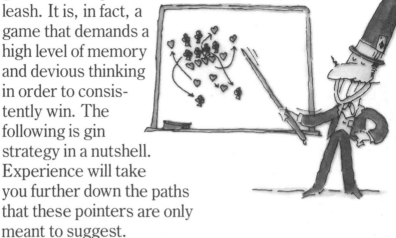

1. Concentrate. Pick up your cards one by one after they've been dealt and focus on them individually. Ask yourself very pointedly, "What do I have? What are my possibilities?" Rummy is one of those games where a little concentration can take you a long way.

2. Be tidy. Organize your hand to clearly show what you've got and what your suspects are.

3. In general, knock as soon as you can. Don't wait for gin unless you're very good, or very lucky.

4. Don't pull a card from the discard pile just to make a pair in your hand. It's usually not worth it. Only pull from the discard pile to complete a meld.

5. Don't toss your aces without an excellent reason. Since they only count one point, they're good cards to keep.

6. Toss face cards early on. Unless you have a good reason for keeping them, get rid of your high point cards fast. (Exception: See next pointer.)

7. If you're dealt a high pair (a couple of kings, queens, jacks or 10s), hang onto them for a few discards. If your opponent has read pointer number six, chances are good he'll toss something useful your way.

8. Analyze the other guy's garbage. You can learn a lot about the other player's hand based on what he discards. Expert players stare at their opponent's discards and ask themselves in detail why that card was tossed.

9. Pick your own discards just as carefully. You can play offensively, and ignore your opponent and what he might need while you toss anything that doesn't fit into your own plans. Or you can play defensively, and hang onto anything that might conceivably be of use to him, even if it hangs up your own hand. Expert players switch back and forth, depending on the stage of the game.

10. Think about tossing a "fish" in the first one or two discards, if you can. A fish is nothing but a brazen effort to fool your opponent about the kinds of cards you're not interested in. (You're looking for a 6 to fill out a threebie of them? And you have a 7 that you don't need? Toss the 7 out. Your opponent will figure that you're not building any straight melds  around the 7, so he might be tempted to toss a 6 if he didn't need it.)

11. Remember what's been played. This is the hardest tip. The pros force themselves to do this. In the later stages of every hand, knowing what's still out there provides a huge edge when you're trying to fill out melds.

CRAZY EIGHTS

♠ Easy to learn

♠ Two, three, or four players
(in partnership) can play

This is right there alongside Old Maid, War, and I Doubt It: one of the basic, don't-start-school-without-it card games. The object of play is to get rid of all your cards.

Let's make you the dealer. If there are two players, give seven cards to the other guy and seven to you. If there are three or four players, give each of them five cards. Take what's left of the deck and put it in the middle of the table, call it the stockpile and turn its top card over. Set it beside the stock-pile and call it the starter card.

Stockpile   Starter card

The player to the left of you goes first and has to lay on top of the starter a card of the same suit or rank. (The starter card is the jack of diamonds? They have to lay on top of it either a jack of some sort, or any kind of diamond.)

If somebody can't lay a card down, because they don't have the cards for it, they have to go to the stockpile and keep pulling one by one until they find a card they can play. All the cards they have to pull stay in their hand.

If they empty the entire stockpile and still can't find a card they can play, the turn passes to their left.

Note one important point: You *can* pull cards from the stockpile when it comes to your turn, as many as you like, even if you *do* have a card that is playable. Once you play your card though, the turn passes.

Those are the basic rules, now here's the story on 8s.

All the 8s are wild. You can play them at any time, whether you have another playable card or not. After you've laid an 8 down, you get to call the next suit, whichever one you happen to prefer, and the next player has to follow in that suit, or, if he prefers and is able, he can follow with another 8. Incidentally, if the stockpile is exhausted, and no one can play a card, the game ends in a block.

SCORING

You can play Crazy Eights game by game, with no cumulative scoring, but most people agree upon some point total, say 100, and work towards it, the winner being the first one there. Points are totaled as follows:

Whoever goes out first scores points depending on how many cards—and what kind—are in the *other* players' hands. Fifty points for each 8, 10 for each face card, and the face value for the other cards (ace = 1 point).

The following are a few pointers on how to be a world class Crazy Eights player.

♠ By far the most valuable cards in this game are the 8s. Unless you think someone is on the verge of winning—and you've no choice but to stop them—keep your 8s in reserve and don't use them until you're ready to make a run at winning. This is often true even if it means digging into the stockpile.

♠ One successful strategy is called "cornering" an entire suit. If you know that most of a suit is still in the stockpile (except for what you yourself are holding), it might be worth taking the whole pile up so as to get every last one. With a corner on a suit, and a couple of 8s to help out, you might be able to empty a hand of 15 cards while someone else, with only three or four in their hand, might be dead in the water. Of course, the key to making this work is knowing how many of each suit have already been played. And that means PAYING ATTENTION!

OLD MAID

♠ Easy, easy, easy, easy, easy

♠ Any number between three and six
  may play with a single deck

How old is this game? There is a cave drawing in France depicting a neolithic family gathered around a stump playing Old Maid. It's a game that's short on strategy, long on luck, and the best part is you get to legally steal cards from your opponent.

BEFORE YOU START

First, take out the queen of clubs and put her aside. Deal the cards around and if someone ends up with a different number, don't worry.
 doesn't matter.

Examine your cards to see if you have any pairs. (Two 8s, two queens... whatever). If you do, pull them out of your hand and put them face down on the table. If you have three of something, you can only lay two of them down. If you have four of something, you can put them all down since they are two pairs.

THE PLAY

When everyone has discarded all their pairs, you can start. The player to the left of the dealer begins. He reaches over to the player on his left and, without looking, extracts a card from his or her hand, and adds it to his. If it makes a pair, he discards that pair, and it's the next player's turn. (If it doesn't, tough luck, it's still the next player's turn.)

Around and around the table it goes, until some poor fool is left holding a single, unmatchable queen (everyone else should be out of cards). That lone queen is the kiss of death and its owner is... the Old Maid.

OH HELL

This is an extremely popular four-handed game that combines two rare qualities: The basics are quickly learned, yet the play can be endlessly complicated for those who like their plots well thickened. It bears a simplified resemblance to Bridge, but there are no partners, everyone plays for themselves, and the rules are (thankfully) far simpler.

BEFORE YOU PLAY

All you need is a single deck. The ace ranks the highest, next king, queen, jack, 10 and so forth.

A single game of Oh Hell is a series of deals. How many deals depends on how many players there are. With four players, there will be 13 deals and that counts as a single game. With five players, there will be ten deals; with six, eight deals; with seven, seven deals.

On the first deal around the table, everyone gets only one card. The bidding goes around, then the player to the dealer's left leads a card by tossing it face up to the center of the table. *Everyone else must follow suit if they can.* The highest card takes the trick, it's scored, the cards are returned to the deck, it's re-shuffled, and another deal is started.

On this second deal, two cards go to each player. Again, the bids are made, two tricks are taken, scored and another deal goes out. This one should be three cards to each player; the next deal is four to each player . . . and on its goes.

THE WAY IT'S PLAYED

After everyone has sat down and a dealer is picked (let's say it's you), shuffle the cards and deal everyone a single card face-down. Then, put the balance of the deck face-down in the middle of the table and turn over the top card. The suit of that card is "trump." *This is done after every deal except the last in a four-player game when the hand is played with no trump.* Incidentally, if you don't know what trump means, read the next paragraph. Otherwise, skip it.

Discards

Stockpile

45

"Trump" is an expression that should have, and maybe even did, come from "triumph." It just means that that particular suit is better than all the others, at least for this deal. If you turned over a heart of some kind, the lowest heart will beat the highest of anything else. In this example, where hearts are trump, your little 2 of hearts will wipe out somebody else's ace of spades. (Of course, if someone else has a 3 of hearts, that beats your 2.) Trumps are the super cards. Play them carefully.

Now for the bidding. On the first deal, when everyone is holding nothing but a single card, it's pretty easy. If you're holding the ace of hearts (hearts are trump in this example), bid "one." That means you think, when everyone lays down their cards, you'll be able to beat them all. And you'll be right. Nothing beats the ace of trumps.

If you're holding the 2 of some other suit, you'll bid "pass" or "zero." That means that you think your card will not be the best when all the cards are laid down. And again, you'll be right. The 2 of something besides trump is as bad as it gets.

The problem arises when (as usual) you're holding some card in the middle. It's not the best, and it's not the worst. If you bid zero and it turns out your card *is* the best, you've "busted." That's just as bad as not winning when you thought you would. The goal is to bid (or "contract") exactly right—not too high and not too low.

Scoring is simple. If you hit your bid exactly right, you get 10 points plus your bid. If you busted (went over or under), you get nothing. At the end of a game, everyone adds up and the winner has the highest total.

Don't forget! Whichever suit is first out in a trick *has to be followed.* If I'm the first one to play in a trick and I lead a spade, *everyone has to play their spades if they have any.* If they don't, they can play any card they like, including, of course, a trump suit.

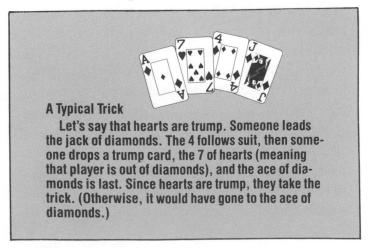

A Typical Trick

Let's say that hearts are trump. Someone leads the jack of diamonds. The 4 follows suit, then someone drops a trump card, the 7 of hearts (meaning that player is out of diamonds), and the ace of diamonds is last. Since hearts are trump, they take the trick. (Otherwise, it would have gone to the ace of diamonds.)

STRATEGY

Things get a bit trickier as the dealing goes on past the first couple. As an example, let's talk about the third deal. The dealer gave everyone three cards and then turned over the top card revealing a spade. So spades are trump for this deal. You're holding the jack of spades, 9 of diamonds and 5 of hearts. How good a hand is that?

It depends. If you bid right, and only win the number of tricks you bid for, it could be a fine hand. If you are too conservative and underbid, or too liberal and overbid, it could be a lousy hand.

Anyway, you decide to bid one. You think your jack of spades, being a high trump, looks pretty good. The other two cards you think you can dump. One of the other players bids one, the other two bid zero. That makes a total of two tricks that people think are going to be won. Unfortunately, there are three tricks in this deal (you're holding three cards), and somebody has to win each one. Incidentally, the dealer is supposed to do this little calculation and announce that two tricks have been contracted and three tricks are going to be played. Moral: Somebody is going to be a bustee for sure.

The player to the left of the dealer leads a queen of clubs. You're next. You don't have any clubs, so you drop your bomb—the jack of spades. The next two players "follow suit" by putting down clubs (remember, if you have a card in the suit that's been led, you *have* to play it).

So you've won a trick, just like you predicted. Congratulations. Now you have to make sure you don't win any more. Unfortunately, everyone else at the table will be trying to make sure you *do* win another trick, so that you don't get any points. Meanwhile, you'll be looking for ways to make sure that those players who bid nothing win a trick apiece, and the player who bid one, never gets it. The bottom line: Everyone is working at cross purposes to everyone else *unless* somebody gets way ahead, in which case it's perfectly legal to gang up on the leader and try to bust her whenever possible.

To carry this example a little further: You won the trick, so you have to lead. You put down your 5 of hearts, figuring somebody has to have a better heart than that. Turns out you're wrong. The player next to you puts out the 3 of hearts, everybody else throws off another suit—not trump.

The trick you didn't want to win is yours

Ouch. You've won another trick and you've busted your contract. All you can do now is lead your last card, the 9 of diamonds, and hope that somebody besides the other player who bid one trick wins it.

This whole deal could have had a happier ending if you had not played your trump first thing. A trump as good as a jack can probably be saved. When the first trick was led by clubs, you should have thrown off your 9 of diamonds, then somebody else has to lead and you'd be holding one lousy card, the 5 of hearts, and one great one, the jack of trumps. At that point, your chances of making your one bid contract would start to look pretty good.

Here are some general rules for play. Like most general rules, they're only good part of the time. Your problem is knowing which part.

♠ A high trump is practically a sure thing. Hold on to it for the first round unless you can't—or have an excellent reason for playing it.

♠ Be particularly alert to "singletons," cards that are all by themselves (in terms of suit), particularly if they are high. Such a card is termed "unguarded" and the best policy is to get rid of it as soon as you can, unless you're counting on it to take a trick (a risky proposition if it's not trump).

♠ Pay careful attention to the other play-ers' bids, and constantly scheme for ways to bust them. If a deal is "overbid," if more tricks are contracted than there are cards to be played, get especially crafty. Somebody's gotten overconfident.

♠ Chickenheartedness is good policy. Underbid more often than overbid.

MICHIGAN

♠ Easy

♠ Three to five players,
  but four is best

Michigan is a good choice when your group runs the gamut in terms of card experience. Since the rules are quickly learned, the fish can sit down semi-fearlessly with the sharks. There's room for a good bit of strategy (although it's far from mind-boggling), and lastly, because it involves the use of a pool of M&Ms, there's the opportunity for a little re-distribution of wealth.

BEFORE YOU START

If you have an extra deck of cards laying around, pull out the ace of hearts, the king of clubs, the queen of diamonds and the jack of spades. (If you don't have an extra deck, just use a pen and four scraps of paper and make believe.) Next, everybody has to bring their own little pile of M&Ms to the table. Or if you don't have any M&Ms, you can use chips or tokens of some kind, but it's not as much fun.

Put the four cards in the center of the table and leave them there. These are your boodle cards. Everybody has to reach into their personal stash of M&Ms and put two on each of these cards, except the dealer, who has to put four. This is known as the ante.

THE PLAY

Dealer distributes the cards starting to his left, as usual, and going around. Sitting right next to the dealer, invisible to all, is the widow. Deal her in just like the rest of the crowd. If the cards don't come out quite evenly, don't worry, it doesn't matter.

After looking at his hand, the dealer may decide to throw it in and take the widow's hand.

He has to do this blind, however; peeking at the widow's hand is not permitted.

If the dealer decides to keep his hand, the widow's hand is auctioned off. Interested parties may bid M&Ms for it. Whoever takes it must then distribute her winning bid amongst the boodle cards.

The player to the left of the dealer is the first to play a card. She may choose any suit in her hand, but she must lead the smallest card she has in it. (In Michigan, the 2 is low, the ace is high.) Whoever at the table has the next highest card in that suit then plays it, followed by the player with the next higher card, etc. Note that the play does not go around the table in an orderly fashion, but instead jumps around depending on who has the next card. Play continues until the ace is played, or if the ace is not available, until the highest card available is played.

Whoever plays the high card in the suit that was led has the privilege of leading another suit (using their lowest card of it) and starting the next go-round. Same as before, everybody plays the next higher card in it until it can go no higher. Incidentally, if one player should have two or three cards in sequence, they must play them all. (I have the 5, 6 and 7 of clubs? And the 4 of clubs was just played? Then I have to lay down my 5, 6 and 7.)

As soon as someone is able to empty their hand, they're allowed to collect M&Ms from every other player. How many depends on how many cards each opponent is left holding. One M&M per card.

But What About the Boodle?

Oh yes. If at any time a card identical to one of the boodle cards is played, its lucky owner is entitled to collect all the M&Ms that were piled on top of its boodle twin, and everybody else has to kick in two more M&Ms to replace those that were taken.

Oftentimes, boodle cards will not be cleared off during a go-round. If that happens, the M&Ms just stay put and become part of the next ante.

HEARTS

♠ Easy

♠ Four players are preferred,
three or five are still OK;
one deck

The game may be played by three or five
players, but four-handed Hearts is generally the
preferred form.

Hearts is one of those ideal card games.
Simple rules, but endlessly complex strategy. It's
simple enough to make it a summer camp basic,
but challenging enough to interest tournament-
level players. In fact, hearts tournaments are
staged every year where the depth of calculation
rivals that of bridge.

As a result of all these fine qualities, it is
an extremely popular card game, particularly
among people who almost certainly should be
doing something else—college students being
the most flagrant example.
For some years now,
hearts has been the
undisputed, number
one card game on
campus. The
variant described
below is the one
usually thought

of as offering the greatest challenge. It's called...

BLACK LADY

The object of Black Lady Hearts is to lose tricks. You don't want to win any tricks that contain hearts, and you definitely don't want to win the trick that contains the queen of spades. There's one exception to this: If you can manage to take *every* trick that contains a heart, and take the queen of spades as well, that's called "shooting the moon" or "slamming." It's very risky, but if you do it, you are richly rewarded.

Here's the way the cards are scored: Each heart counts 1 point against the player who takes it, while the queen of spades counts 13.

If four players are at the table, deal 13 cards to each. If an odd number are playing, throw out some small cards to equalize things. (Three players? Throw out the 3 of clubs. Five players? The 3 of clubs and the 2 of diamonds.) Ace is the high ranking card in hearts, everything else following as per usual.

Everyone inspects their hand after the deal and then selects three cards to give to another player. You have to pass your cards before you can look at the cards you're receiving. Rotate the direction of the pass on every deal (left, right and across) so you're not always passing to the same person.

Whoever is holding the 2 of clubs begins the game by leading it, and play continues to his or her left. To lead a card, all you do is take it out of your hand and place it face-up in the center of the table. Like many trick-taking card games, hearts demands that all players follow the suit that was led—if they can. Since clubs are always led in the first suit, players following *must* drop a club, unless they can't because they don't have any. If they can't, they can drop any suit (discard any card) *except* a heart or the queen of spades.

A Typical First Trick
The 2 of clubs has been led, the jack, 10 and queen all follow suit. The queen takes the trick and the queen's owner now has the lead for the next trick. Note tendency to dump off high cards.

After the first trick, this rule changes and you can play the queen of spades anytime you're able.

Here is the last basic rule: No one may lead a heart until one of three things has happened. Your hand is entirely hearts, hearts have been "broken," that is, discarded onto some other led suit, or the queen of spades has been played.

A trick is taken by the person who lays the highest card on it *in the same suit as the card that was led.* The winner of a trick leads the next trick.

If no one is able to follow suit on a trick, the person who led keeps the lead. There are no trump suits or wild cards in hearts. It's a very democratic game.

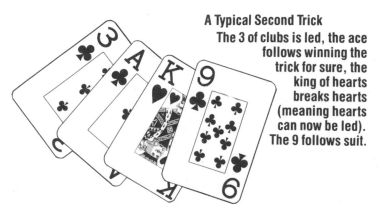

A Typical Second Trick
The 3 of clubs is led, the ace follows winning the trick for sure, the king of hearts breaks hearts (meaning hearts can now be led). The 9 follows suit.

Here is how the scoring goes after a deal is over (with four players, that translates to mean all 13 tricks have been played and taken):

Players count the number of hearts they ended up with and that number goes in their column. Whoever ended up with the queen of spades has to add 13 points. If someone was successful in shooting the moon (winning all the hearts as well as the deadly queen), they subtract 26 points from their column.

After a pre-set number of hands (deals), columns are tallied up and the winner has the smallest total.

A Typical Third Trick

The 4 of clubs leads. The big queen falls, meaning this player has no clubs. The ace of hearts falls, meaning this player also has no clubs. The queen of clubs takes the trick, meaning this player is now the proud owner of 13 points for the queen of spades, and another point for the heart.

STRATEGY

The woods here are pretty thick and entire books have been written on nothing but hearts strategy. What follows is a beginner's collection of tips and points. Once you play hearts very long, you'll start to work your own way down the twisty roads that lead off from this simple set of rules.

♥ **Pointer One:** If you're dealt the queen of spades, pass her on unless you have at least three and preferably four other spades as well.

♥ **Pointer Two:** The same is true for the ace and king of spades. Get rid of them unless you're well covered with lower-ranking spades.

♥ **Pointer Three:** Don't pass any spade lower than the queen.

♥ **Pointer Four:** If you receive the queen of spades on a pass, try to dump her off as soon as possible.

♥ **Pointer Five:** High hearts are also prime passing candidates, only a little less certain than the top three spades.

♥ **Pointer Six:** Before the pass, but after you've looked at the top priority suits (spades and hearts), take a look at the minor suits, clubs and diamonds. You should worry about them if they're completely "top heavy," that is, if they contain nothing but high cards. If they're balanced, if they contain both high and low, you should be all right. And, of course, if they're bottom heavy, they're golden. But if you're looking at the king and queen of diamonds or clubs, all by their lonesomes, I'd think seriously about passing them on, or you could find yourself the proud owner of the queen of spades very shortly.

POKER

At last. Here we are at the dark heart of American card games, poker. Much has been said over the years about the family of card games that go under the general heading "poker." Untold fortunes have been won and lost and entire lives have been spent in the sweaty-handed pursuit of poker pots. Not that much is absolutely certain about the game since it lives in the world of calculated odds, but two things can be said with 100% certainty: It is far and away the most popular and least-liked set of card games in America.

The source of the game's appeal and controversy lies in the fact that, as currently played, it has become an adrenaline exercise with money supplying the critical element of risk. Central to the game is the ability to bluff an opponent out of a deal, by raising the risk factor too high for him. Standard draw or stud poker can get a little dull if bluffing becomes impossible, as it often does with penny-ante games. (As proof, you might put your hand on your pulse and say the words, "Raise you 40,000 M&Ms." Now, leave your hand in place and substitute the word "dollars" for "M&Ms.")

The mixture of money and odds is, of course, the devil's recipe and a good bit too rich for my blood. Around here, we play for M&Ms, but with an added kicker that varies from game to game. Some examples: Winner gets ice cream, loser cooks dinner, loser forfeits dessert, loser has to pledge everlasting devotion to winner... things like that. Risk perception, after all, is a personal value and don't be embarrassed if a pot of 14 peanut M&Ms gives you all the shakes you feel comfortable with.

Think of it this way. High-stakes poker is like tightrope walking over Niagara Falls. Poker with match sticks is like walking on the cracks in the sidewalk. M&M poker with pre-agreed penalties is somewhere in the middle, depending. Pick the elevation that works for you, but the rest of this discussion will be directed for those of us who like it just a few feet off the ground.

Poker Hands, and Which Beats Which

Poker has entered into American folklore to the point where the values and names of the poker hands are in the dictionary and everyday language. Even if you never intend to play a hand in your life, you should learn the following information as part of your lifelong course in essential twentieth-century American street culture.

Although there are thousands of ways to get there, depending on the variant being played, poker games almost always end with a "showdown," where all the players still left in the deal reveal the cards they're holding. This is the Big Moment when the cowboys used to  stand up and accuse one another of cheating. Just exactly which hand beats which is described next, in descending order. We'll assume that none of the cards are wild. And in poker, the ace is a wonderful card. It can rank either high or low, going with either a 2 or a king. You'll see what I mean in the descriptions below.

Royal Flush. Ace, king, queen, jack and 10 of a single suit. The ultimate hand. Completely unbeatable. And almost completely unattainable. (The odds of ever receiving it on a single deal from a well-shuffled deck are 1 in 649,739.) This is the kind of hand you get on the same day you win the Irish Sweepstakes.

Straight Flush. Five cards, all of the same suit, that are in rank sequence. Another hand from fantasyland. Beats anything except another straight flush with a higher card. The best possible straight flush is a royal flush: ace, king, queen, jack and 10. The worst possible is 5, 4, 3, 2 and ace. Note that the ace, great card that it is, can go with either the king when it's high or the 2 when it's low.

Four of a Kind. Four cards of identical rank. A great hand, one that you might even get someday. Beats everything except the rare hands described above. In a matchup between two players, both holding four of a kind, the higher cards win.

Full House. Three identically ranked cards, plus a pair, also matching in rank. A very fine hand, bet the rent on it, sometimes. Beats all hands except the above; and in a matchup with another full house, the highest trio wins. (You're holding three queens and two 5s? And he's holding three kings and two 4s? Sorry, he wins.)

Flush. All five cards are the same suit. Rank doesn't matter. Another excellent hand. Beats all hands except those above. In a matchup with

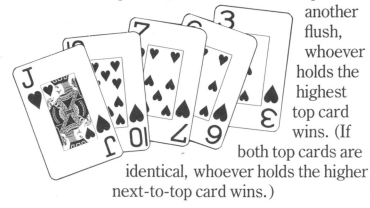

another flush, whoever holds the highest top card wins. (If both top cards are identical, whoever holds the higher next-to-top card wins.)

Straight. All five cards are in order. Suit doesn't matter. Good enough to lose you a lot of M&Ms when someone else manages a flush. Beats all hands except those above; in a matchup with another straight, she who holds the best top card wins. Don't forget the schizophrenic nature of the ace. The best straight is the ace, king, queen, jack and 10, and the worst straight is the 5, 4, 3, 2 and ace.

Three of a Kind.
Three cards are
the same rank.
Suit doesn't mat-
ter. The other two
cards are orphans,
they don't match
anything. Beats all
hands except above; in a matchup with another
three of a kind, the better cards win.

Two Pair. Like the name
says, two
matching pairs
of cards. The
suit doesn't
matter. In a
matchup with
another set of
pairs, he who has
the top pair wins.

air. Two cards that match in rank. Suit
n't matter. A lowly hand, although every

poker player in the world will be happy to tell you about the fortunes they have won with nothing but a pair and a good bluff. In case of ties, the next ranking card determines. (You have two aces and your next best card is a jack? And she has two aces and her next ranking card is a 10? Collect your M&Ms.)

High Card. Last and least. If there are no combinations of any kind in your hand, you have a lousy hand. Its highest ranking card is all you have in a showdown. In case of ties, the next ranking card determines.

In the rare event that the two best hands in a showdown match each other right down the line, the pot is split.

How to Bet

There are only two fundamental things you have to know in order to get started on any of the thousands of poker games. The first is how to rate the hands (see above); the second is how to bet.

After the dealer shuffles, he or she offers the deck to the player on their right to cut. This is customary and probably dates from Wild Bill Hickok. In the middle of the table lies a pile of chips (or M&Ms, if you're playing at my place). This pile is the pot, and it got there because everyone had to ante a chip into it in order to be included in the deal. The ante is your ticket to ride. It's non-refundable.

Each game has its own wrinkles, but the basic pattern to all of poker goes like this. Card or cards are distributed and a betting round begins, at which time players have several options; bet, pass, raise or fold (don't worry about what it all means, we'll get to that in a minute). This pattern repeats itself a set number of times until the showdown, when players reveal their cards and win or lose, or sometimes split, the pot. That's the rough idea; here is how it works in one of the most popular poker varieties.

FIVE-CARD DRAW

♠ **Four to ten players**

Originally, in prehistoric times, poker players were dealt five cards all at once.  They stared at them for a while, and then bet them or "folded" (quit). The players who were left then had a showdown and the winner took the pot. Good enough for the cavemen perhaps, but not quite exciting enough for the modern thrill-seeker.

Nowadays, in the basic version, players are dealt five cards, the bets go around, and then they get the chance to improve their hands by discarding as many cards as they don't like and replacing them with top cards from the deck. Then they bet on their new (improved?) hands. The conventions of betting are a little tricky, so pay attention to this part.

The player to the left of the dealer goes first. Let's say it's you. You've looked at your cards, thought very deeply, and now can do one of two things: bet, or pass. Simplest is the pass or "check," as it's called. It means you're still playing, but not placing any bets right now. Second option is the bet. You like your hand. You take some of your own chips and add them to the pot. How many? It depends largely on your confidence level. A bet means you think, when all is said and done, that your hand will be the best at the table.

If you check, the player after you has the same two options—bet or check.

If you bet, you've "opened the pot" and the player following you has different choices. He can fold, call, or raise you—but he can't check. Folding, as you might guess, means he puts down his cards (unrevealed) and sits the rest of the hand out. "Calling" simply means the player puts in the same number of chips you did, and no more. "Raising" means he puts in the same number of chips, and then adds some—in other words, makes his own bet.

Once the pot has been opened in a round, players can no longer check. In order to stay in the deal, it's going to cost them—at a minimum, they have to match the bet that's just preceded. Even if a player or two have folded rather than match someone's bet, when it comes around to your turn again, you have to look at that bet and choose: fold, call or raise.

Theoretically, this could go on forever, around and around as people raised one another, but the ʳule is generally only three raises per round, no matter who makes them.

The round is over when:

♠ Everyone has checked.

♠ Everyone has answered (folded, called or raised) any bets. The only limit here, as I said, is three raises per round.

After the first betting round is over, players get a chance to improve their hand via the draw. This is the modern wrinkle that separates us from the cavemen. Here is how it goes:

Take a look at your cards, and decide how many of them you want to keep. Maybe you like all of them. Maybe you're holding a royal flush. In that case, keep them all. But, on the other hand, maybe you're holding nothing but trash— with the possible exception of a lone king. In that case, put the four rejects face-down on the table and ask for replacements. The dealer will oblige. Although rules vary on this point, in most circles you can discard any number of your cards. All of them, if you like.

Your hand before the draw. Only one card shy of a flush. You toss the diamond, ask for a new card and...

...get no help. You now have a trash hand. This is typical.

Now take a look at your new hand and see what improvements you've wrought. Another betting round is about to begin and it will soon be decision time again. Betting in this new round generally follows the same rules as before.

Some games insist on a betting limit, i.e., a maximum size to any individual bet. Others will install two limits, one before the draw, and one after. The after-draw limit is generally higher than the before-draw limit. Before you slap a 15 M&M limit on your game though, reflect on the strange-but-true fact that limit games frequently generate far scarier pots than no-limit games. I think it's part of the same psychology that makes drivers particularly careful on no-limit autobahns.

In any event, once this last betting round is over, it's time for the showdown. Put your cards on the table.

SEVEN-CARD STUD

♠ Two to ten players

Stud poker differs from draw poker in one key regard: Half of your cards are no secret. They're lying wide open on the table for all to see.

At first, this doesn't seem like such a swift idea, giving away half your secrets. But it actually has a reverse impact. Looking at half of someone's hand is highly suggestive, but far from conclusive. And into that gap between suggestion and reality you can pour a lot of M&Ms.

After the customary shuffle and cut, the dealer distributes two rounds of face-down cards, then a round face-up. Everyone peeks at their face-down (or "hole") cards with no expressions permitted. Then a round of betting starts. The player with the best showing card begins it.

The rules for betting are the same as described earlier, in poker basics. In brief, as the bet comes to each in turn, players can either call, raise or fold. The pass or check option is only available when no bet has been made in a given round. After a bet has been made (the pot has been opened), players have to at least call it to stay in. After every betting round, the pot closes and when the next round starts, you can, once again, check until someone re-opens it with another bet. A round is over when everyone has checked, or all raises have been called.

After everyone has bet, another three cards are dealt around. All of them are face-up, and a betting round goes between each. The last card, the seventh, is then dealt face-down and followed by a final round of betting.

And remember, although you've got seven cards, all you're looking for is the best five-card poker hand.

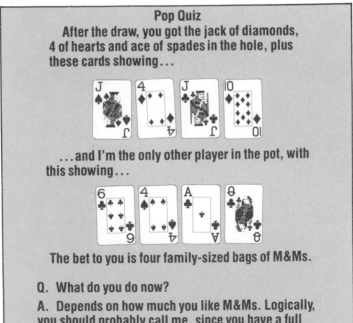

Pop Quiz
After the draw, you got the jack of diamonds, 4 of hearts and ace of spades in the hole, plus these cards showing...

...and I'm the only other player in the pot, with this showing...

The bet to you is four family-sized bags of M&Ms.

Q. What do you do now?
A. Depends on how much you like M&Ms. Logically, you should probably call me, since you have a full house (three jacks and a couple of 4s), and I've got nothing showing. With your luck, though, I'll have three queens in the hole, beating you with four of a kind. On the other hand, maybe I'm bluffing... Send in your M&Ms, and I'll let you know.

STRATEGY

I don't know of any ironclad rules in poker strategy, but I do know that no one else knows any. The heart of the game is odds (read luck) and despite what you've heard, nobody knows the odds in such a way that they can always win. After having read the brief description of the rules given here, you might very well beat the World's Champion over five or six hands. (Quit immediately, if you do.) Over a little more time the pro's experience would quickly start to tell, but luck plays that kind of a role.

BLUFFING

Let's say you're looking at a mediocre hand (as usual), say two pairs, 8s and jacks. Four other players have gone through the draw and three are still in the deal. The bet to you is a full 15 M&Ms. With four hands still in contention, your pairs are probably not the best at the table. But you can, if you choose, try to bluff some of the rest of them out by calling those M&Ms and raising another 15. Look calm during this. If you're lucky, you might be able to run a few of them out of the pot, maybe even all of them. Bear in mind, however, an old saying which I just made up: Show me a poker player who bluffs all the time, and I'll show you someone who doesn't have very many M&Ms.

General Guidelines, or
A Little Knowledge Can
Be a Dangerous Thing

What follows are general play guidelines, nothing more. Once you've played the game a while you'll begin to see what kinds of hands are winners, and that information will begin to accumulate into your own set of guidelines. In the meantime,

♠ Don't play very many hands. If there are five people still playing in the pot with you, the chances of your having the best hand are only 20%. This is a sobering realization, but the implication is obvious: You should fold a good bit more than half the time.

♠ Don't read a lot of minds. Not unless you're a time-tested psychic. Play your cards, not your opponents' shaking hands. And in the same vein, don't underestimate any of the other players. (After all, they were smart enough to pick you as an opponent.)

♠ Don't bluff a lot. While it is certainly true that the M&Ms you win with a lousy hand and a bone-crushing bluff are always the sweetest, you should use a great deal of restraint in this area. There will be times when an Academy-award winning bluff will be a smart play, but those times are not nearly as frequent as most beginners think.

♠ Forget the M&Ms that were once yours but are now the pot's. Those M&Ms are gone. Erase them from your mind. Treat every bet as if it were your first.

♠ Last, and most obvious, never play poker with a man called Slim.

SOLITAIRE GAMES

Despite what you've believed all of your life, solitaire is not the name given to any single game of cards. It is, rather, a family name. According to Albert Morehead and Geoffrey Mott-Smith, probably the two leading solitairians of our time, there are some 250 distinct games that fall under the category solitaires.

The most common of them, a game called Klondike by Morehead and Mott-Smith, is actually a rather poor example of the type. It relies almost exclusively on luck, it takes too long, and it's very hard to win.

Fortunately, with 249 others to pick through, far better solitaires can be found. For example, the three described next are (personal opinion) vastly superior. They are all played with a reasonable mix of luck and skill, they don't take more than 10 minutes to play, and your chances of winning vary a great deal depending on how you play.

Of course, as a result of all these fine qualities, they are all completely addictive. If you have anything like a compulsive personality, a fondness for crossword puzzles, or even an unusually large number of lonely nights, any of these games could be dangerous for you.

KLONDIKE

I'll include the rules to this, the most common solitaire game, if only for old time's sake. As I mentioned above, it has no business being as popular as it is. (If these rules don't make any sense, ask the person sitting next to you. It's that kind of game.)

THE LAYOUT

Shuffle your deck exceedingly well and make seven piles as illustrated. All the top cards are face-up, all the cards underneath are face-down. The pile farthest to the left has only one card in it, the pile next to it has two, the next pile has three, the next, four . . . and so on to the last pile with seven in it. Leave room on the table just above these seven piles to create four more. The seven piles we'll call the "layout"; the top four we'll call "foundation piles."

THE BASIC IDEA

The object of the play is to get all the cards up to the foundation piles. Each foundation pile contains only one suit. It is started by the ace and has to be built in order from there: ace, 2, 3, 4... up to king.

A card is "available" for play if it is at the top of one of the layout piles. (See illustration for what is meant by top.) If an ace is exposed in the initial setup, you have to move it up and start a foundation pile. Then turn the newly exposed card face-up.

On the layout, build down from the exposed card in alternating colors. (A red queen is showing at the top of one of the layout piles? You can overlap it with a black jack as shown.) As you build like this, you'll create columns of

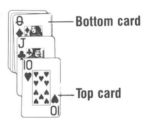

— Bottom card

— Top card

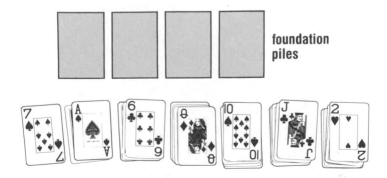

foundation
piles

A typical layout

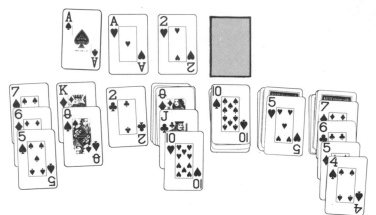

Same layout after a couple of plays

half-overlapping cards that go red/black/red/black ... going down in order of rank.

All the overlapping face-up cards on a pile can be moved *as a unit* whenever the face-up *bottommost* card will play somewhere. (You've got a red queen/black jack/red 10 showing? You can move all three of them, as a unit, if a black king is available for play somewhere.) If an ace turns up, you must move it promptly to start a foundation pile and turn over the next card.

Whenever all the face-up cards of a pile are cleared off, turn up the next card; it becomes available. A space made by clearing off an entire pile can be filled only by a king (plus any cards that happen to be built off the king).

When you turn up (in your stockpile) a card that can go onto the top of the foundation piles, it can go straight there.

THE PLAY

Turn up the cards from the stockpile (what's left of your deck) three at a time. In other words, peel them off the deck like this: face-down, face-down, face-up. The face-up card is available for play. You can go through the stockpile as often as you like this way, although as cards get played into the layout, the stockpile will obviously diminish.

Once a foundation pile is started by the ace, you can add to it whenever the right cards become available. Note though that you don't *have* to do this immediately. You might like to leave them in the layout for a while to see if they can help with the maneuvering of the cards. (This is practically the only part of the game that involves any judgment at all.)

You know you've won if you can get all the cards off the layout and onto the foundation piles. The chances against you, incidentally, are something like 30 to 1. Good luck.

YUKON

In keeping with our mysterious Alaskan motif, this next game is called Yukon. If there were any justice in this world, Yukon would be the standard game of solitaire, not Klondike. It is a far superior game. Your chances of winning are a tantalizing 1 in 4, and you can do a great deal to improve or hurt them by proper play. Playing time, incidentally, is under 10 minutes.

THE LAYOUT

Start the same as for Klondike. Deal 28 cards in seven piles; all the top cards should be face-up,

This is a typical layout

88

all the others, face-down. The leftmost pile has one card, the others go up one at a time from there ending with the last pile containing seven.

With the remaining 24 cards (and here is where it differs from Klondike) deal them face-up evenly upon all the piles except the leftmost, the single card pile. Half-overlap these cards, so that you can see what every face-up card is. You'll be left with no stockpile, all the cards being in the layout.

Above the layout will be space for your four foundation piles, exactly as in Klondike. You'll be aiming to build these foundation piles in the same suit starting with the aces and ending with the kings.

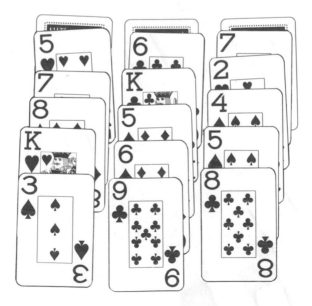

The Basic Idea

The object of the game is the same as Klondike. Build all four of your foundation piles completely. Cards can be moved up to the foundations only when they are at the top (remember what "top" means?) of a layout pile. Builds are made with cards of opposite color, and next-lower rank. (You've got a red 8 at the top of a pile? The only card you can play on it is a black 7.) So far this is identical to Klondike, but here comes the big improvement.

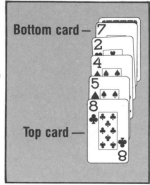

The Play

In Yukon, *all* face-up cards are available for building onto other layout piles. If a red queen is at the top of one of your layout piles, you can move any black jack onto it that you can see, no matter how deeply buried it is. When you move it, however, all the cards that are covering it are moved as well.

If an ace is cleared off at any time, you have to move it immediately up to start a foundation pile. However, any other card which could be played onto a foundation pile (i.e., it's the right rank, right suit, and is located at the top of a layout pile) can be played whenever you like. In a lot of cases, it makes sense to keep such a card in the layout for a while, because you may need it there. The trick is knowing when to move it onto a foundation pile, and when to keep it in the layout.

If any pile is completely cleared off, it can be re-started only by a king. You can use any king in sight, as long as any cards that are covering it come with it. Any face-down card that becomes completely cleared off should be flipped over; it is now available. One of the strategies of the game is to flip over all face-down cards as soon as possible, and you should bend your tactics in that direction.

These gray
squares...

will
be where...

**We made one play off our typical layout
(p. 88/89) and got this...**

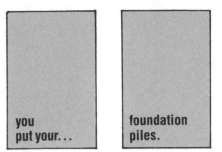

you
put your...

foundation
piles.

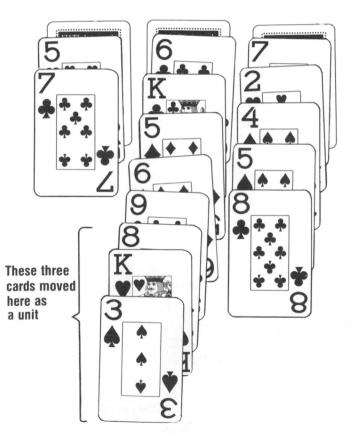

These three
cards moved
here as
a unit

Wayne Miller/Magnum

BRISTOL FANS

This solitaire is a mutated version of Grand-father's Clock and one of the Klondike games. But it ends up being more interesting than either, mostly because it moves so quickly. Smart play will make a big difference in how many games you win, but if you end up batting .500, you're doing a little better than average.

THE LAYOUT

Deal eight fans of three cards each, all of them face-out, as illustrated on the next page. If any kings show up, move each to the bottom of its fan. (Note I said "bottom.")

Below this main part of the layout, deal a row of three face-up cards, starting the reserve piles.

Give yourself some room around the fans, since you will be adding to them as the game goes on.

THE BASIC IDEA

As aces become available by reaching the top of a layout or reserve pile, you'll be moving them to a row above this layout where they will start four foundation piles. These piles have to be built

UP from ace through king as the cards become available. Always build with the next card higher and don't worry about suit. It doesn't matter.

On the layout piles, you'll be building DOWN from kings through 2s, always using the next-lower card. Keep in mind the reverse directions here: Up on the foundation piles, down on the layout piles. And also keep in mind that suit doesn't matter.

This is a typical layout. The three bottom cards are the reserve piles. Note the king of spades was moved to the bottom of its pile.

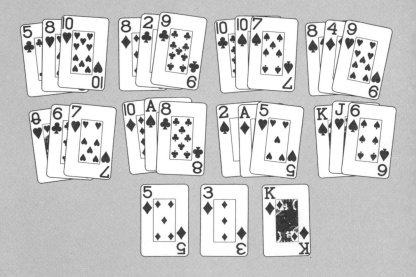

THE PLAY

All the top cards of the layout fans and the reserve piles are available for play. If they're the right cards, they can be moved onto foundation piles, or onto other layout piles. Only one card at a time may be lifted off a fan, or off a reserve pile. You cannot add to the reserve piles by taking cards off the layout piles. Fans can be built up to any size.

The same layout, after having done all the possible moves. Two foundation piles, started by aces, are in place. Time to deal three more cards onto the reserve piles.

Whenever you decide you need some fresh blood, you should deal three cards face-up onto your reserve piles—one card onto each pile. Even if you should empty a reserve pile, keep its place open and put a card there on the next deal. Stop between each deal to play whatever cards you want to. Do not fill any space in the reserve except by the next deal, and if a fan is completely emptied, it is never re-filled. Also, there is no re-deal. Once you've gone through your whole deck, that's all you get.

Some Strategy

There can be a distressing amount of planning in this game. How you move cards, or even if you move them, are decisions that have to be pondered. The only thing the rules force you to do is move the aces immediately as they become available. Every other legal move is up to you.

The main problem you want to avoid is reversals (think of them as "tangles") in the layout or reserve piles. If some low cards get buried underneath some high cards, that can create an "immovable object" when you start to build up your foundations. Sometimes you can eliminate these tangles simply by moving cards around the layout, and that's the preferable way to do it. But other times you may be forced to build up a big foundation pile in order to clear out one of these roadblocks. You'll just have to figure it out through experience.

GRANDFATHER'S CLOCK

Your chances of winning this solitaire are quite good, probably something like 3 out of 4. On top of that, there is plenty of opportunity for proper choice making, and it plays in less than the required 10 minutes. However, the real reason I'm including Grandfather's Clock is that you'll never be able to remember how to lay it out without keeping this book around.

THE LAYOUT

Just look at the illustration on the next page and match it exactly. The 12 cards are supposed to represent the numerals on a clock. The 9 of clubs stands at 12 noon; all the rest follow as shown.

Below your clock, arrange the remainder of the cards as shown in eight columns of five each. All of them go face-up.

THE BASIC IDEA

The object of the game is to build onto the cards in the clock until the right card is at the right clock position: At the 9 o'clock position, the top card should be the 9; at the 4 o'clock position, the top card should be the 4, etc. For the purposes of this figuring, the cards are valued like so: Jack = 11, queen = 12, king = 13, ace = 1 and every-

The cards in the clock have to be exactly as illustrated. The cards in the layout are just what we got in our shuffle.

thing else is face value. The basic idea of building cards onto one another is borrowed from Klondike and you can look at that game if this explanation doesn't make it clear.

Note the following key point. When you are building cards onto one another, the ace can go either below the 2 (as usual for solitaires) or above the king. This makes the ace a particularly valuable building block.

THE PLAY

The top card of any layout pile is available for play on any available clock card, or on the top card of another pile. An available clock card is the top card of the pile. The building goes UP on the clock piles, and DOWN on the layout piles. As usual, the cards have to go in order. The suit doesn't matter, and you don't have to alternate colors.

If you clear off a whole pile, the space can be filled by any available card.

Because of the fact that the ace does double duty in this game, going below the 2 *and* above the king, you can do the following neat things. Let's say a 2 becomes available on one of the layout piles, and you want to build on it. The ace is your only card, since the ace goes under the 2. But if a king becomes available on the clock, and you want to build on it, the ace is again your only card, since the ace goes above the king.

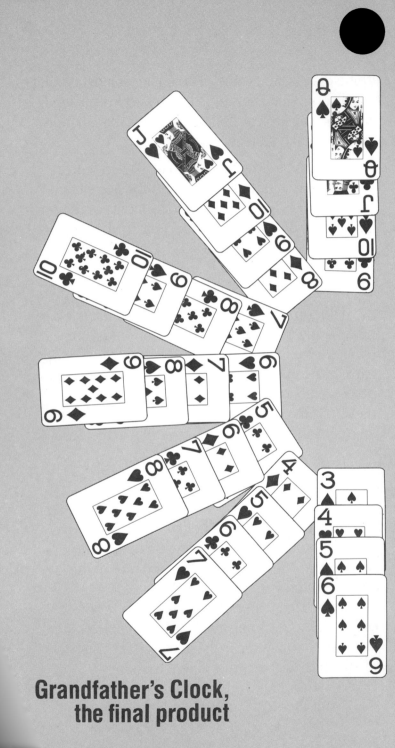

**Grandfather's Clock,
the final product**

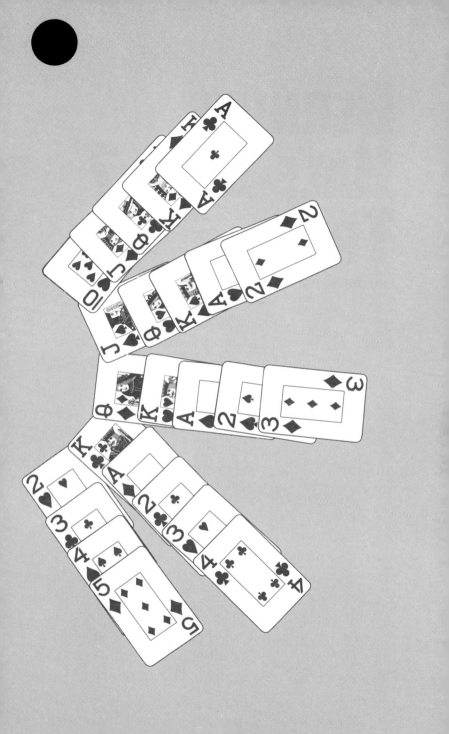

103

BERNIE'S HALF-DECK 7 TRICK

A no-brainer card trick. If you can count and remember one card and one number, you can pull this one off. Unlike most "self-working" card tricks though, this one is actually pretty good.

As always, the secret is the show. If you just collar a volunteer and then walk her through the steps toward the grand finale, you're never going to get that big call from the Tonight Show.

As you're shuffling a deck elaborately, explain that you've just been shown an interesting card trick which requires a volunteer. Not just any volunteer, however; it requires someone with extraordinary mathematical abilities. As you finish saying that, grab a likely looking candidate and ask them to begin turning over cards and putting them into a pile while they count out loud. Explain that this is a test; you are going to be listening for errors.

When they get to the seventh card, memorize

it, but don't stop them until they get to 26. ("That's fantastic. Absolutely error-free. Incredible!")

Let your volunteer tidy up the 26 cards she's counted out, then you should take them back, turn them back over and put them on the bottom of the deck.

Flip up the top three cards and put them face-up in a row, like solitaire columns. Why? It's a secret. You're going to build three columns of cards that total 10 points. For the purpose of this little exercise, figure any face cards, including the ace, at 10 points. Everything else goes at face value.

Building these columns shouldn't take any time. If a face card is up, that column is already worth 10 points, so it's finished. If any other kind of card is up, say a 6, put four *face-down* cards below it, each of them half-overlapping the next. That makes your 10. (If a 5 is showing, put *five* face-down cards below it, etc.)

In this layout, "X" = 23. (You'll understand when you read the next page)

Make sure no one, yourself included, sees the face-down cards.

During this little process, explain that you are ordering the cards so that all the cards on the table total 16. Sixteen, you should explain, is the number of pyramids located on the Egyptian "Plain of Dead Souls." Oftentimes, of course, the cards won't total 16. If anyone points that out, brush them off.

Once all three columns are treated this way, made into 10 pointers, *add up the value of the face-up cards and silently memorize that number.* Let's call that number "X."

Now tell your victim to deal X cards off the top of the deck and put them into a stack. All the cards that are in columns on the table can just stay there. You won't be needing them anymore.

Here's the trickiest part. Remember, at the beginning of the trick I told you to memorize the seventh card that was turned over, back when your volunteer was turning over 26 cards? Well, now's the time when it matters.

When she's finished the pile, the top card, the last one she dealt, is the one you've memorized. Take that pile, put it on top of the rest of your deck, cut it and shuffle—*making dead sure the memorized top card stays on top.* This is not difficult. Just finish the standard shuffle with a little extra care.

Now you have a fully shuffled deck, except that you know what the top card is. How you reveal that little secret will make all the difference in how this trick comes off. Here are a couple of options:

1. You can use the "sticky pinky" routine that is described in the Trickier Card Trick on the next page. Turn the deck so its back is to you, ask the deck to give you the memorized card, and if you wave your forefinger over it properly, the deck should oblige, at least it will if you've read the directions properly.

2. Or, a simpler option: You can pick the card up, and without looking at it, put it against your volunteer's ear. Then look into her other ear and read the card through the vacuum. This is my favorite.

A Trickier Card Trick

This is a seriously amazing card trick which you should practice in the privacy of your own room before trying on anyone. The moves aren't too difficult (they wouldn't be in this book if they were), but a little time spent in front of a mirror is highly recommended. Don't worry though. It's worth it. Pull this off properly and you can just about retire.

The Effect

What the audience sees.

The magician (that's you) allows a volunteer to inspect a deck of cards, shuffle and cut it millions of times and then return it. The magician then rif-

fles through the deck, puts it up his shirt (read that part again), and asks his volunteer to cut to the 6 of diamonds ("Just take some cards off the top of the deck, it's not hard, any number you want"). The volunteer cuts the deck by grabbing some cards through the fabric. The magician then removes the remainder of the deck from under his shirt, and then, by waving his finger over it very carefully, the 6 of diamonds is seen to rise on its own from the deck. At no time is the magician seen to touch or look at the card.

The Real Secret to This Trick

Classy presentation. Make a whole show of it. If you just march up to someone, tell them to pick a card, and then presto out it pops from the deck ... you'll have wasted a good effect.

Much, much better is to weave a story around it. Play the role of the beginner magician to the hilt (shouldn't be too hard under the circumstances).

You don't really know how to do this trick...
you saw it once on TV but it's been awhile... you
think this is how it goes. Fumble with the cards
at first. You might mention that it's not really a
trick since it relies on static electricity, but still
it's interesting...

Make sure that this role of fumblethumbs that
you're playing is just that—a role. Practice the
real moves of the trick in front of a mirror very
carefully. They're not difficult, but that doesn't
mean you can't do them wrong.

The Other, Less Important Secret

1. Position yourself in front of an audience so that
    no one is behind you, or to your side. If you're
    sitting down, and your audience is standing,
    that's perfect. Take your deck of cards, ask
    someone to inspect it, shuffle it, cut it and give
    it back. Then hold it out as illustrated. Start
    talking about how much you're worried this
    trick isn't going to work.

2. Give a volunteer the following instructions:
    "Take this deck of cards, shuffle it millions of
    times, then give it back to me." After you've
    gotten it back, riffle through it, noting that the
    top card is the 6 of diamonds (or whatever...
    just don't forget it). Then add the following
    afterthought: "Maybe you should cut it too.

But here, I shouldn't see anything... I'll close my eyes. No! I have a better idea! I'll stick it up my shirt *and* close my eyes."

3. As you put the deck up your shirt, discreetly turn it upside down. Ask your volunteer to grab a bunch of cards through the fabric and cut to the 6 of diamonds. ("It's not hard, really. Just grab any number you want.") After they've cut once, but before you take the cards out, get fussy and don't settle for it. Get them to re-cut the deck. ("Go with your instincts. You're thinking about this too much.")

4. Now, as you pull the bottom half of the deck out, flip it back so that it comes into view wi the backs on top. If you did this correctly the top card (the 6 of diamonds in our examp. e) is still the top card. Tell your volunteer to just drop his half of the deck on the floor ("Go ahead, make a mess").

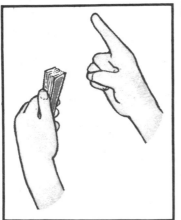

5. Hold your part of the deck as illustrated. They're looking at the face of the bottom card, you're looking at the back of the top card. Time now for some serious shenanigans.

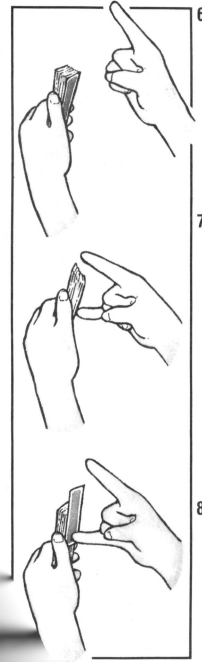

6. Rub your forefinger in your hair and slowly bring it down to the deck where you should begin to wave it very slightly over the deck. Talk about the miracle of modern static electricity.

7. When your forefinger is pointed at the audience, and waving slightly over the deck, your pinky is invisible since it's behind the deck. Take advantage of this little fact and stick your pinky out so that the end of it is touching the back card of the deck (the 6 of diamonds).

8. Now, as you wave your forefinger ("filled to the brim with static electricity!") over the deck and begin to raise your hand, the back card will come

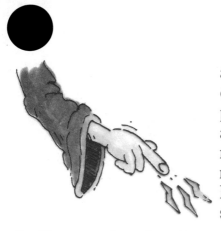

along—courtesy of your sticky little pinky. To get the appearances just right, spend a little mirror time with this. It's a fabulous illusion. Don't muff it.

9. To strengthen the effect, as the card is just coming into view, you can put your hand back up to your head and "recharge your forefinger" by rubbing it through your hair again. Just make sure you get your pinky back into its innocent place whenever your hand is in full view.

10. Once the 6 of diamonds is half-revealed, you can just grab it and pass it over. Ask very innocently if that is indeed the correct card ("amazing stuff, static electricity").

11. A final note: Do not ever, ever, ever repeat a trick or give it away. Legions of dead magicians will haunt you if you break this single rule.

Complete Plans for a Modern Three-Bedroom House of Cards

FIND A FLAT, LEVEL SURFACE FREE FROM DRAFTS AND BREEZES. THE STEADIEST HAND AND MOST PATIENT EFFORTS CAN QUICKLY BE DESTROYED BY A SUDDEN GUST OF WIND, REDUCING YOUR CARD HOUSE TO RUBBLE AS IF HIT BY A TEXAS TWISTER.

ACTING AS THE CONTRACTOR, FOLLOW THE BLUEPRINTS TO BUILD THE HOUSE OF CARDS. OF COURSE, IF YOU FAIL, YOU WILL PROBABLY, LIKE MOST CONTRACTORS, CURSE THE ARCHITECT, TOSS THE PLANS IN THE TRASH AND BUILD IT YOUR OWN WAY.

WHILE TRUE DYED-IN-THE-WOOL CARD HOUSE BUILDERS WOULD SCOFF AT THE IDEA OF USING BENT CARDS,

AS AN ARCHITECT I NATURALLY LOOKED FOR WAYS OF MAKING THE STRUCTURE MORE STABLE AND BELIEVE THAT IF YOU SHOW ME A TRUE DYED-IN-THE-WOOL CARD HOUSE BUILDER, I WILL SHOW YOU A PERSON WITH TOO MUCH TIME ON THEIR HANDS.

ANOTHER TIP IS TO LEAN THE CARDS AGAINST EACH OTHER SLIGHTLY, LEAVING A GAP AT THE BOTTOM, THIS WORKS BETTER THAN TRYING TO PLACE THE CARDS IN A PERFECTLY VERTICAL PLANE.

MANY OPPORTUNITIES EXIST WHILE CONSTRUCTING YOUR HOUSE OF CARDS TO ESTABLISH YOUR PERSONAL SOCIO-POLITICAL BELIEFS, FOR INSTANCE, MAYBE YOUR HOUSE REFLECTS YOUR PREFERENCE FOR THE PARLIAMENTARY SYSTEM OF RULE, PLACING THE KING & QUEEN AT THE TOP OF THE HOUSE SUPPORTED BY THEIR ROYAL COURT

BELOW, OR PERHAPS THE HOUSE IS MADE ENTIRELY OF
COMMON CARDS, THUS REFLECTING YOUR BELIEFS IN A
TRUE DEMOCRATIC POLITICAL STRUCTURE. THEN AGAIN
MAYBE IT'S JUST A HOUSE OF CARDS AND YOU'RE
JUST LOOKING FOR A WAY TO KILL SOME TIME.

BEGIN AS ANY CONTRACTOR WOULD BY USING THE
FOUNDATION PLAN TO LAY OUT THE BASE CARDS
PROPERLY, COORDINATION BETWEEN THE PLANS AND
ELEVATIONS IS ESSENTIAL TO PROPERLY CONSTRUCT
THE HOUSE.

MONTGOMERY ANDERSON A.I.A.
CODY ASSOCIATES, ARCHITECTS

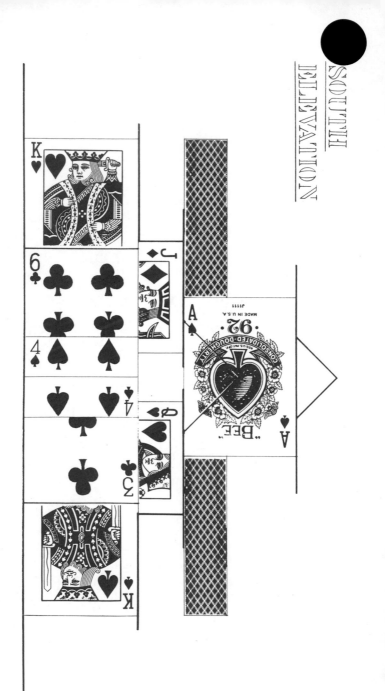

PLAN KEY

H   CARD PLACED HORIZONTAL

V   CARD PLACED VERTICAL

FOUNDATION
PLAN

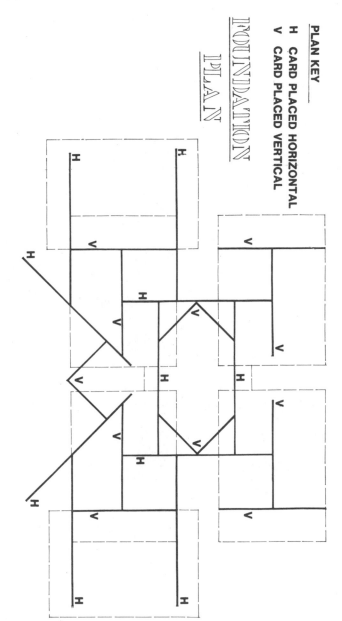

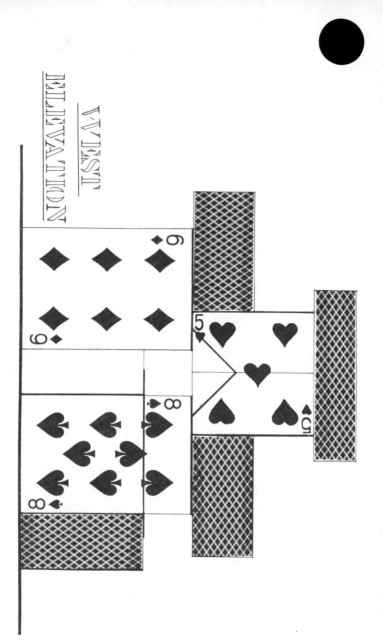

ELEVATION

WEST

EAST
ELEVATION

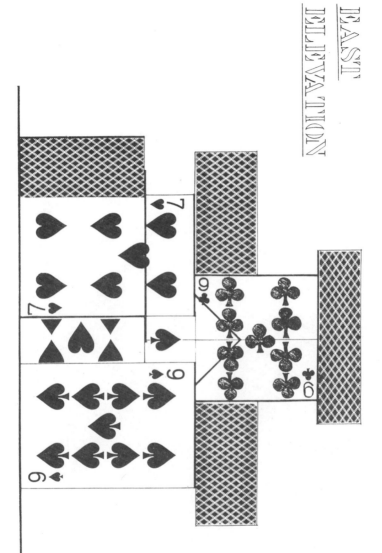

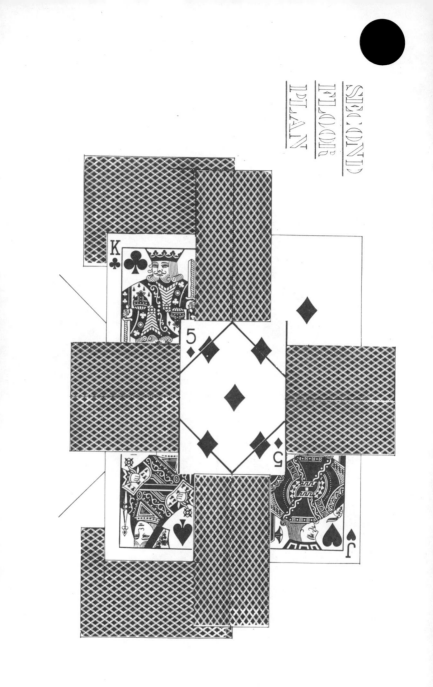

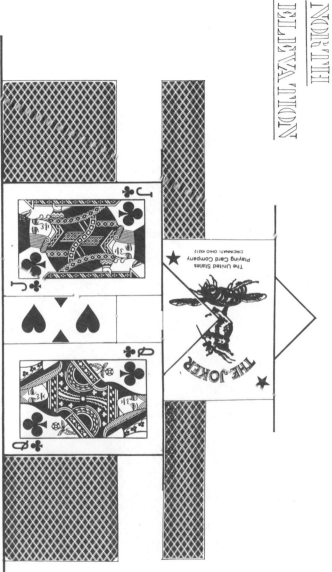

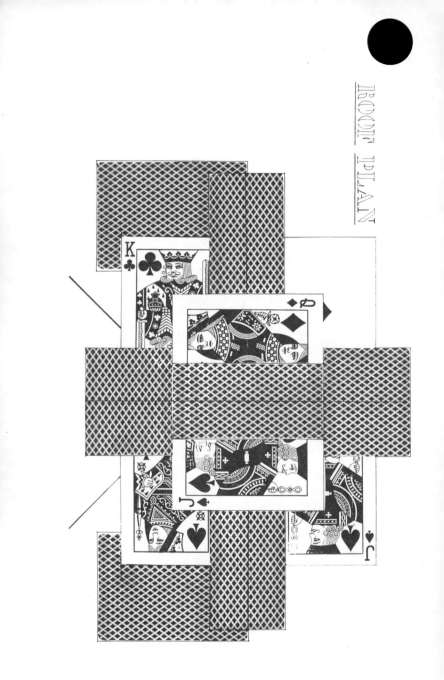

CREDITS

GRATEFUL ACKNOWLEDGMENTS:

Robin Winston
Michael Stroud
Howard Schwartz
Wayne Schmittberger
Bob Ciaffone
Monty Anderson
Alan Adler

CARTOONS:

Ed Taber

INSTRUCTIVE ART:

Sara Boore

COVER AND CARD ILLUSTRATION:

David Clark

COVER AND CARD DESIGN:

Mark Eastman

BOOK DESIGN AND PRODUCTION:

MaryEllen Podgorski
Suzanne Gooding
Linda Harris
Ann Shumway
Lisa Venditelli

MORE GREAT BOOKS FROM KLUTZ

The Only Activity Book You'll Ever Need

The Book of Classic Board Games

The Klutz Book of Ball Games

Cat's Cradle®

Coin Magic

The Etch A Sketch® Book

The Footbag Book

Juggling for the Complete Klutz®

The Klutz Book of Magic

Potholders and Other Loopy Projects

Stop the Watch®

The Spiral Draw Book

Table Top Football

KLUTZ.com
Come on in!

OPEN 24 HOURS

CAN'T GET ENOUGH?

Here's how you can keep the Klutz coming:

1. Get your hands on a copy of **The Klutz Catalog**. To request a free copy of our completely compelling mail order catalog, go to **klutz.com/catalog.**

2. Become a Klutz Insider and get e-mail about new releases, special offers, contests, games, goofiness and who-knows-what-all. If you're a grown-up who wants to receive e-mail from Klutz, head to **klutz.com/certified.**

If any of this sounds good to you, but you don't feel like going on-line right now, just give us a call at 1-800-737-4123. We'd love to hear from you!